Nort

th of

YESYES BOOKS PORTLAND

Order

NORTH OF ORDER NICHOLAS GULIG

NORTH OF ORDER © 2015 BY NICHOLAS GULIG

COVER ART: "SIX STICKS" © 2015 MICHAEL KENNA
COVER AND INTERIOR DESIGN BY ALBAN FISCHER

ALL RIGHTS RESERVED. NO PART OF THIS BOOK MAY BE REPRODUCED WITHOUT THE
PUBLISHER'S WRITTEN PERMISSION, EXCEPT FOR BRIEF QUOTATIONS FOR REVIEWS.

FIRST EDITION, 2015
ISBN 978-1-936919-15-4
PRINTED IN THE UNITED STATES OF AMERICA

PUBLISHED BY YESYES BOOKS
4904 NE 29TH AVE
PORTLAND, OR 97211
YESYESBOOKS.COM

KMA SULLIVAN, PUBLISHER

HEATHER BROWN, PUBLICIST

MARY CATHERINE CURLEY, DIRECTOR OF SOCIAL MEDIA

MARK DERKS, FICTION EDITOR, *VINYL*

STEVIE EDWARDS, ACQUISITIONS EDITOR

ALBAN FISCHER, GRAPHIC DESIGNER

JILL KOLONGOWSKI, MANAGING EDITOR

JOHN MORTARA, WEB DESIGN AND MANAGEMENT

PHILLIP B. WILLIAMS, POETRY EDITOR, *VINYL*

JUSTIN BOENING, PROJECT EDITOR FOR *NORTH OF ORDER*

JOANN BALINGIT, ASSISTANT EDITOR

BEYZA OZER, ASSISTANT EDITOR

AMBER RAMBHAROSE, ASSISTANT EDITOR

CARLY SCHWEPPE, INTERN AT *VINYL*

ROBERT WHITEHEAD, ASSISTANT EDITOR, *VINYL*

FOR MY PARENTS

"… here I can see // you."
PAUL CELAN

CONTENTS

I

THE CRY WAS IRREVERSIBLE   *15*
THEN THE EVERGREENS   *17*
IN YOU THE SKY ANNEALS THE LIVING SHALLOWS OF   *18*
OUTSIDE // OF IT   *19*
CAME TO, PLACED BY THIS LOCALITY   *20*
THAT SEPTEMBER THERE WERE NOISES IN THE BUSHES &   *21*
LATER, INSECTS SPARK THE ROAD   *22*
WITHOUT ADDRESS THAT YOU   *23*
IN INCREMENTS // THE WATER TURNS TO SILT   *30*
AS IF THE RADIUS   *31*

II

BEYOND THE LIVING   *35*
HARDER NOW THAT THERE ARE CENTURIES   *39*
FOR SEVEN YEARS I   *42*
OCEAN EDGED, THE ENERGY IS THAT THE CONTINENTS DIVIDED   *43*
THUS, THE WATER DRIVES // ITS ERROR UNDER   *44*
NORTH OF ORDER // NORTH OF LIGHT   *45*
TERRORSTRUCK, A ROW   *52*
BOUND &/OR EMBODIED   *53*

III

PUSH & PULL OF WE, OF STARTING OVER IN THE OFF   *65*
EARTHWARMED   *66*
OUT OF REACH   *67*
GUT MOAT, BLACK BOAT, HARBOR   *69*

PLUMMET FORWARD, PLUMMET PAST   *70*

HUNGERED INTO   *71*

ACROSS AN IRRIGATED FIELD, THE WIND A BELL   *72*

TROUBLED INTO   *81*

EDGING INWARD // A MONUMENT   *82*

EVENTUALLY YOUR MOUTH BECOMES A HOLLOW WRAPPED   *83*

ARE YOU NEAR ME? A LIGHT HAS SWEPT   *84*

HERE, THE GROUND IS WHERE THERE ISN'T. NO BREATH BEYOND   *85*

ENDING OVER IN THE UP   *86*

IV

TURNING & TURNING OVER   *89*

THUS // THE BRANCHES   *100*

AS WHEN A FOREST // PRESSED   *101*

CONNECTED   *102*

FROM THIS VICINITY   *106*

BREAK OF LOOKING, GLASS & GODWORK   *107*

IN YOU A LANDSCAPE   *108*

BELL-STRUCK, WATER-STRUNG, IN THIS   *113*

ACKNOWLEDGMENTS   *115*

THANK YOU   *117*

NORTH OF ORDER

I

THE CRY WAS IRREVERSIBLE. // We couldn't place it, couldn't call it past the black hills, the white hills.

I tried // to bring it near me, cupped my hands around

                                                          the air as though to draw
from water // the center of the river up.

Within it all the lilacs withered on // their branches, the wild vines. It fell

upon the city like a veil, invisible although   I felt it, the opposite of landlocked,
                                                         parallel

to sea. // I closed
my windows, all my doors.

What entered us // erased us. It shattered through

                                                       the cracks. A static off
the mountain // turning echo, turning

drone. // Had I been able then, less filled by all I held & couldn't bury

I would have told you   after matter, after fact // your face became the glass through which I wanted

what I watched. I placed my arms around you, waited. // You said to me, we're fine

THEN THE EVERGREENS // released. Windbite.

You were emptier

than trees. The blue black grass

pulled open at the edges of // the field

repeats the field's

intelligence. Repeat to me

the water you are under // moving over stone

IN YOU THE SKY ANNEALS THE LIVING SHALLOWS OF the water, the push & pull

of forms // a fall of birds
have failed to shadow

down. // Switchgrass in the iron meadow.

Octagons of pollen. Burnfield writhing in the pine

OUTSIDE   OF IT // to you I said
I thought   to seed

a higher field from which in you to fall // you said

from far // enough to love
From fall

                                    to fall I spoke in you
to bare

a world within   us breaking
                                      rarely seen // the trees

that you and I

                                    are speaking (a wooden chord
                                      unquiet

CAME TO, PLACED BY THIS LOCALITY. Peopled. In the underbrush our bodies shaded further into making, made. To look upon ourselves beneath the water. There among the current & the faces & the reeds. Incompletely met, approachable. The locality swarmed around us. It teemed. Breathed & didn't breathe as we did. For years, we watched it & we wanted & we waited. We placed our bodies in because of

                                                      (we walked upon the land

THAT SEPTEMBER THERE WERE NOISES IN THE BUSHES & we believed them. Birded

but unnamed.
                                                               You took me where the willow // strangled

in its vines & violet
flowers // eroded on a concrete shore,

                                               the ragged grass. // I couldn't love you.
You took away

the place where every knife is silver.
                                                                  (the anti-

field

LATER, INSECTS SPARK THE ROAD that leads in nine directions. It isn't summer anymore // not even

in the imagination.
How many // words for what

a landscape turns to
                              air when you believe it water where // you're from

WITHOUT ADDRESS THAT YOU   & I (in mind) this morning

in a city   we imagined

startled
stood without

       a word you backed against
       the window

partially dark // I stared

& stared upon your face became // an avenue
       in snow // the opposite of ocean

       mostly physical
       the sea in us but only mostly

Once we heralded			the tiny births inside us (low
					explosions) making

day & day				etc.
a smaller death				the taste

					within
					of wanting

you to spell // the buildings pressed between us // planted

The city that you were // the sound we washed

in brine
away each other by

                                      ourselves a throat
                                      to hold

                                      above
                                      the boulevards

to cast them off completely still // did I believe the sprawl

was other than
                                      the water

Cold   the way a breath
                                                         is cruel

Unusual the land without a once // within the trees to name

the streets pedestrian
We walked   together
                                                         & were not

                                                         among the others // thus ourselves

Unnoticed & not locatable

                              the porous

shore // in faith
a bright   reversal //
                              the opposite

of not
that you are   here // that I am
                              Is it enough

to break apart &   open
                              barely // only

once // & live together in // the wake of having

having heard it
a way to claim our eyes   are starving for
                              a form

                              (a single
note imagined

                              writhing through us // waking (into
                              error, wreck

Harder now
& colder   the city living

art of what would you turn into
                                        here

That we occur (in   this) That we
                             within

the mind the
thought of wanting now

                             to do to you
the thought the

mind   would never in the open want
                             to constellate

the merely // physical the mess of beauty made of many
                             faces // stranded sea of none

                             of whom without
                             our eyes

we fall apart

                        to know (a place not far from where

                    the river

IN INCREMENTS // THE WATER TURNS TO SILT by mid-September & there is nothing

                                                                left that we can separate from stalk.

It isn't getting easier.

From where your voice decays I watch you hook around yourself

a bracelet bent from silver

                                                              partially opened // a circle

hanging from

                                                 your wrist

AS IF THE RADIUS expanding // expands the landscape

outward (the empty oval of

your mouth // opening

and my mouth (an ocean pulled

apart (our eyes

in awe // the waves

expanding // a wreck of birds, expanding

II

BEYOND THE LIVING   edge // a field emerges
stitched together
      your voice is made
of grass // a tree   in the wilderness // discrete

      listening
      to see

        the ground within us
withers. Do you
remember? No one sung
to me of me except the shore I sung to // thinking
how in this distress
        to burden, or
        to bloom. The winter
ripped the needles from

                      the branches // hung
in mid-December   opened
bare as I
could make them
       up, the sky
a sea of white
that failed // to break above us

     senseless, yes, but
blooming in
& further // the field beneath
the sky was wild,
    an after-
      form in which
a forest formed around us   & went out

HARDER NOW THAT THERE ARE CENTURIES // before us, forests

felt // We, oblivious.
We, in clamored depth of what

      there is
to see dissolve

the ground & water
further under // How should I erase you?

The sky is not
       my sky

is not upon me
readily. Though I have made you

Maker // the world
a fledgling

instance we have formed // & found it useful not
to bind my hands

together, or
to speak, what is it here that fires through

                                                & cinders?
I do not believe

around us burning
the ruined this in which the simple thought

that we belong among the going &
                    the gone disproves the harvest

fully after
matter, after fact.

What is it in us now we've learned to live without

& how should I
beside myself // a deafening of pattern &

                             of place //
believe it in me to resume?

It isn't useful here to tell you pines do not disintegrate
in winter. From fire, or

from seed // In snow
the needles stay // I was once without you,

once in tow

FOR SEVEN YEARS I followed, writhing

in your wake. // Higher up, I held the ends of branches stripped

of bark. I wrapped

the bark around a stone. I dropped

the stone in sea. The sea

encircled, ruptured (the shallows rose // up slowly

OCEAN EDGED, THE ENERGY IS THAT THE CONTINENTS DIVIDED. Cell Light, Nightshade, Ardor.

                    If I could place my eyes within my mouth upon you I would cease // in nine directions building

            monuments of air upon
               the inshore.

Even in their furrows
in their rows

                              the recent gods // are jagged.
                                In this of which we are

through what
material // crowsong off the aspens pulled because we listen

THUS, THE WATER DRIVES   ITS ERROR UNDER // heaven
                             under // ground

I miss you terribly despite myself // the violence of
                             a recent

                             fever, faith

a form for air through which
                             the sky you said // would never

NORTH OF ORDER // NORTH OF LIGHT

      we woke the groves

we spoke in

wind   the wind was all

around us // even ragged
> flecks of bark made autumn by

the scrape

of rutting deer collected

on // the floor we walked away
& stopped
       our reason for
a moment there were only

seven // flowers I could organize
        correctly four
of which were
        barely   red

enough to memorize the sun   dissolved
                the muscles of
your back // your arms your
shoulders held   the weight illuminated

I couldn't stop the want
heretical in me // & swarming down
   upon the under-
forms of roots you crossed

above & left upon   the path behind you
broken by   your passing I
      awoke // the lesser
field was audible, out of   answers, reach

  TERRORSTRUCK, A ROW of starlings echo off
          the branches // scattered.

You have filled my mouth with lavender.
         Circle, are you near me?

I am near the river where it hurts,
the Middle Sea.

But I have hungered   blindly. Are you near me?

         Believe that I
am fire glassing forests

        (the rapt intelligence of faces
staring

        upwards // out

BOUND &/OR EMBODIED // the flesh a light

is hesitant // the half

shut window // a form of water

falling in a dark house

blinking // the day against // the glass

Stranded clearly // black

on either side disintegrating // into place

places we imagine

in us // before a field is // made // the thing itself

until the story we

have told ourselves to order

our position // embedded in the visible // particulates of stone

Fallen into & away // if we are speaking

of each other

incorrectly of ourselves // a place

for air to stress

between us matter into // matter further fact

& it has happened // is still

happening the bright light // animal until

animal // until the fall through which

we separate // un-gardened // no stone // an occurrence in the mouth we

witness // a body

formed around // the history of surfaces // the horror of

& we have carried in our hands together

the water // & we give a little of it over

to each other

an imperfect gesture, but

what else until // we take it

place it // back into a garden // a growing field we turn

in order to belong

the fractured pattern // happening among appearances

Because to watch is to participate

the dead material // day-

dried // shards of bark in increments the green

grass the deep // green

shadows // branches of the burr oak // leafless

twisted through // our eyes haven fallen shut the sun

itself has fallen

sufficiently a center for another // self a home if we

are present in our

houses // the blank interiors of walls

That we have built together

bearable // burning without rehearsal

near the fire

here // or soon to be

to feel alive the heat that rises out to keep me

near surrender // shards of off

white stone // unlit // the palm as one would keep a portion of

a precipice reverberated back

Imagined the living forest

entered // emptied

the middle of

periphery // a sound the form I dreamt to interlace

preceding each

of us // our impermanence a curtain

made of winter

shaking white

in elms // weighted

the branches crack

to pieces in the mouth the weather

insufficiently transparent // the aperture of things

Only that it might be audible

the restless surface

of the water // vulnerable

the languages existing

there // discernible // as in a field // what is it

then // that thinking is

within the center of // itself

my hand // within your hand if it is possible // in this I

offer // it again the cry

of stone & // oak &

sand // here I // here am // & there are not even

stars above the garden

ash-light // mercy of each other to // be seen

III

PUSH & PULL OF WE, OF STARTING OVER IN THE OFF. Not in this world, nor in any I. Land of talk & circumstance. We gathered up our things. A unity of stones to string together, scatter. A language, then, of that. There, over. Shine a brighter, be because of where the sea is ringing out & in the people. A politic of soil, water. Politic of not, a place in us the ocean took to forming. The shore before the shore

(before the warmer air

EARTHWARMED, the inshore edges past the wrack-line & continues.
What the ocean is

between us // dark wave, bright
                wave, water.

Sailcloth,
hold us closer.

Igniting sheaves of heather
in our boats

                (among the laurels & the driftwood & the rye

OUT OF REACH   beneath // the sea
                                I hear

the further canopy // can you believe // the brittle almost

                                beautiful // I'm not o.k.
                                the first

belief that I remember // breaking now
                                a working form for us

as if to fill // to fall
apart within   a field

of effervescent windows // no two panes of glass alike exactly

                                Though the terror breaks
the terror you & I

we've felt // enough to base upon or place
                                together // jointed

past our aperture
to be alone // in any absolute too early please it hurts enough

to praise the height

of trees   the movement we

resolved to never turn away the higher // shape of leaves

                               among the isn't anything

exactly what I mean

GUT MOAT, BLACK BOAT, HARBOR. An oasis in the forest forged between the rocks. From the outer shore we watch

the higher limbs
              go slack. // In wind

the jewelbirds scatter further. After
answer, after

                                    absolute. // The pattern of their leaving
                                                              leaves us

less than certain
we return.

If there were voices here, I'd stitch their quiver to // my wrist. The water that
                                                                                       there isn't

evaporates regardless
of the river

pushing through us we believed in.
                                        Such stillness breaks the center

of the lake.
For you, I've stopped my diving

PLUMMET FORWARD, PLUMMET PAST. In name, the garden of your asking, a great erasure. What is left to save

in me your voice disintegrates, the base of weed roots
                                          being torn.

Let the sleet rain plunder where it will.

                                          My eyes have seen // the far shore
                                          there asunder

after flower, after bell. Would that through // the world
                              our error joys

                                          a floodplain spilling through us.
Shepherd us if not

to where the river drives // its water under

HUNGERED INTO, the nest in which the bird eggs cease to hatch beseeches that we cinder. Light

the rafters
light the wooden edges of the house.

                                        Use us, Method, to fire further under.

Yellowing the waxwork.
                                                    A brittle ringing, shell

ACROSS AN IRRIGATED FIELD, THE WIND A BELL unraveling // a falling
sea. Of light   interrupted filaments.
The pasture splits
apart // in fertile moments
                of recovery isolated crests becoming multitudes

Derelict, the swollen edges of the bay
                in sudden bursts // porous
margins, our alluvial.
        As if the corrugated glass could shatter
clearly. Coral-white
in shards // the fleeting spark

Witness of the nothing-star, the mineral embankments
        opening // capillary pull
to deepen. Cloud-shade notwithstanding
measurement, the
cracked   perimeters of stone // border of
the shoreline, driftwood
          turning in the gray
rot. The evaporated field   has lessened

Into air   a single name precisely
fallow, drawing
upward in
       the black. Order-northern,
nothing-south // One goes at times into the miracle of fact.
Is never ready

Transparent torrent, the wrack-
line vanishing
in spray // the bracken promised to its shadow.
       Disintegrating
veins, scattered yellow // leaves

To imagine Burr Oak   Quercus, Northern White

a person would have to gather

back the fragments

       in their arms

would have   to say it over to

           themselves // to other islands

(a dust beneath us
             drifting. The ground
dissolves // a long way back into its center

Unsteady silt, deep green

waves   of salt. Depleting

        to believe // a row of exits, the washed out corridors

of rock, the climate of

our listening

Insisting rain does not
           become us // bedrock, star. In fields
                      of limestone
oceans. The eroded openings
of groves
                   the eye looks out
alighting   pitch, the constellated trees

TROUBLED INTO

sentiment // a blank material, the un-

real sky
within the body

vaguely human
(the here inside the I inside the am

EDGING INWARD // A MONUMENT of air // the sea, a field emerging. Is it true from this

we make our houses?
I am standing

in the center of the space your shadow works behind you

                                        turning // in a circle
forming shore

EVENTUALLY YOUR MOUTH BECOMES A HOLLOW WRAPPED around your finger when you think // before

                                                            the words come out

a halo, or a nimbus
or a ring. // When the inscape echoes

past the edge-line // a border opened // What else if not the sky

ARE YOU NEAR ME? A LIGHT HAS SWEPT the aster's center. Flattened calyx. Clustered, a rare cacophony

                      of birds // circling. To me you look like something sorrowed into I have touched.

Drone-song swarming through the aspens, a world
                      of pollen, wind

HERE, THE GROUND IS WHERE THERE ISN'T. NO BREATH BEYOND // the forest. No vocalist as if the birds emerging

off the branches // furthered
into fracture.

Nothing
here, I hear it. Your name is not

the world of things
I sing

ENDING OVER IN THE UP. Of air, the air that left the middle. Ground. An atmosphere that entered & encompassed & grew thick. The land became beneath, became the edges of the water, errored and/or, traced. We teemed around it & we listened. Sang & didn't. Although we wanted, thought. Although accordingly we couldn't. What was it there for us, or for itself, a settling. To cast a net of reeds in which the sea disfigured every roughness

(post-perennial, after the affair

IV

TURNING & TURNING OVER, an acre made of faces we have hacked our voices through the trees, leaves the color of your wrist. I loved

                                                the taste of water then. I told you many times // the rain, a way

to empty.
No loud clap

                                    of thunder, no chorused order claimed by what the ground eroded into, a murder of red // birds pouring

                                                      down the mountain

In sand our bodies collapsed as if the braided strings were severed. The color of rye wheat, red meat. Your wrist was like the seven skies stitched shut around

a lakebed dried to nothing.
By September, a unity

of landed fish.
& the part of me made modern to

become // became

Nightshade notwithstanding, your current garden drapes across the ground. Beetle husk & splinter.

Because you press what's palpable in you as though to shatter
        through into another // form, the vagrant variations. I find it violent

to believe. Spit
the river out. Would that there were voices

                                      made of forests we
could harvest ardor in. I

the blind distributor
of I. You

                                to fall apart inside of // listening, to see

I'll say it to you once & only, if we are finished here, let's at least evaporate in style. Math & malady. Math,

                                                    the absolute. The strangest part of staring through the body, feeling the real energy. In the Middle Sea, my name is counting backwards from

the far point on the horizon. // Until I get to three.

Your name
is // the opposite

of the open space on either // side of anything that's west. Sand, the color of our numbers

Face the landscape, face the porous shore. I had wanted bloodshed in the bright
pavilion, the weight of bodies

metallurgy, war. // The kind of violence moves me is the prettiest
release. Fist the garden.

In the time of what is left   to mourn, the trees where I was born
more shaped by sun than yours

                                                                                         a darker bark. There
there. The land is turning

over & // we know it.
Pollen fallen off // of lavender. Waterswept.

                                                                                                         The very
                                                                                                        little leaves

& when the river edges past us, to say through you the water is enough. Landlocked

we abandon anything that rings. Meaning, we are ringing.

Meaning, we
are made. // Would that I could tear you from

the delicate. The sound of field
$\qquad\qquad\qquad\qquad\qquad\qquad\qquad\qquad\qquad\qquad$ birds rotting

To spell within a place, a person. Please, I beg you, enter. Erase me here before the forest. Green // white

                                                    brown // blue. I am the son of the son of the son of. // Take me where the river hurts, the Middle Sea

is past me somehow emptied of its motion. Avalanche & valley. Beyond the plastic roses & the hickory, a crooked acre

you have spilled (from frailty
a faith

through what I've formed
in you, a place

our hands
together making // oceans out   of oceans // out of walls

& when the shoreline turns away from us & when the shoreline turns away

yours is the body &
the aperture

the floodplain & // the flower & // the blood

Bear the high woods further

(discordant order,
 guttural

alarm

Counting backwards from the far horizon, I arrive at the sound of &. My own voice counting. Name me

Middle, name me
                                                            West // the kind of modern

water falls upon
to joy // the working forms

of faces
                                                            waving in the wheat

Asterlight & attar // the weight of speaking plates the wilted pistil. What is audible around us falls apart as if a forest

warped by glass.
Look, see // we are locked

in nine directions. Voices of the red birds, far birds, wheat. The body you. The body you release

a ringing // sea
of trees

                                                                       to face
                                                                      around me

places you
have wintered in & patterned after

number // minus number   minus // snow

THUS // THE BRANCHES
bending

                                                down into the horror of
                                                          your mouth

(& I believe you

AS WHEN A FOREST // PRESSED to sky becomes the

sky // becomes

the altered edge, a sea in each interior

(in every open

field an ocean echoes // alters

inward, enters

CONNECTED at the level of the artery
        the level field
in which arranged
the drying corn   was alien

in red we wept
        a death to weave
between the haggard stalks
our eyes

the recent gods could see
          in veins the symmetry
of logic cut
within a center I

could take your hand & point
        to where the farm
land falls apart
& pulls us there, to pieces

FROM THIS VICINITY, I thread a violence through you // trusting what you are erases both of us. // In mid-September

                        we watch the slant light find us making monuments

of bell-grass // a world

                                          of distant figures, rain

BREAK OF LOOKING, GLASS & GODWORK, it happens that we stop. The sea, too, stopping. The fallow field as well, the hollow sky. There, the inscape. There, the living error, answer &/or ache. Mercy, or return. What matters is what falls apart & starts again from clamor, a harbor darkened, the shore of somewhere further off. Edged by anything that's on, we'll keep. If I am leaving here, if you are, make of us a place in which to vanish, a wreck of birds emerging. Real &/or imagined. I swear to you I've seen them. Their shadows pull together, blooming inward, pooling. Upon the body of the actual, opening

(an entrance, or an exit, or an out

IN YOU A LANDSCAPE // collapses through me

Unusual // the symmetry

                of trees

Flooded over // in the past tense // field & terrorflower

(for it, for it is not

                In increments around itself

                              the arc of night

an acre set // adrift in the

        interior

Burning in the middle

                    distance, grass // encompassing

the fence // The hills

                              discretely scattered

Here   & here // the water echoing

the water //
Crows are carrying

         the lake

BELL-STRUCK, WATER-STRUNG, IN THIS that we diminish. Half of what we longed for takes a hatchling shape

        among the fractured casings.
            Cast about

& scattered. Lift the outer up. There has always been a desert // here // no need to rip our hair

upon the mountain.
For years we waved our skinny arms like flags.

                I did & didn't love you. // We fall away

ACKNOWLEDGMENTS

I would like to thank the editors of the *Colorado Review* and *Manor House Quarterly* in which sections of this poem have previously appeared, as well as the US Fulbright Scholar Program for providing me the time and assistance to work through much of this.

THANK YOU

Endless gratitude is due, first and foremost, to my family, Arthur, Toi, and Carla, for their love & their support.

Thank you also to my teachers at the University of Montana, the University of Iowa, and the University of Denver. Particularly Joanna Klink, Robert Baker, Peter Gizzi, Elizabeth Robinson, Dan Beachy-Quick, Geoffrey G. O'Brien, Rod Smith, Bin Ramke, Eleni Sikelianos, and Graham Foust.

Thank you Tony Gulig and Richard Bell.

To my classmates at Iowa and Denver for your attention and advice. Andrew Wells, Adam Roberts, Steve Toussaint, Ally Harris, Cody Rose Clevidence, and Jane Wong, thank you. Serena Chopra, thank you.

To my friends in Wisconsin, when I was younger. Bradley Baumgartner, Bill Hogseth, Josh Macknick, Riley Hartnett, Ryan Olson, Ian Wallace, and Andrew Christopherson. Nicholas Butler and Nikolas Novak, thank you.

In Missoula, Dawn Anderson and Jeremy Smith.

Special thanks is due to Colin Cheney in Bangkok for guiding me through the later stages of the book when there was no one else.

Justin Boening, most generous editor, who built this book beside me, thank you.

To KMA and everyone else at YesYes, thank you.

Finally and most of all, for everything, I would like to thank Numfon Pondongnok.

ALSO FROM YESYES BOOKS

FULL-LENGTH COLLECTIONS

I Don't Mind If You're Feeling Alone by Thomas Patrick Levy
If I Should Say I Have Hope by Lynn Melnick
some planet by john mortara
Boyishly by Tanya Olson
Pelican by Emily O'Neill
The Youngest Butcher in Illinois by Robert Ostrom
A New Language for Falling Out of Love by Meghan Privitello
American Barricade by Danniel Schoonebeek
The Anatomist by Taryn Schwilling
Panic Attack, USA by Nate Slawson
[insert] boy by Danez Smith
Man vs Sky by Corey Zeller
The Bones of Us by J. Bradley
[ART BY ADAM SCOTT MAZER]
Frequencies: A Chapbook and Music Anthology, Volume 1
[SPEAKING AMERICAN BY BOB HICOK,
LOST JULY BY MOLLY GAUDRY
& BURN BY PHILLIP B. WILLIAMS
PLUS DOWNLOADABLE MUSIC FILES FROM
SHARON VAN ETTEN, HERE WE GO MAGIC,
AND OUTLANDS]

VINYL 45S

A Print Chapbook Series

Pepper Girl by Jonterri Gadson

Bad Star by Rebecca Hazelton

Still, the Shore by Keith Leonard

Please Don't Leave Me Scarlett Johansson by Thomas Patrick Levy

No by Ocean Vuong

POETRY SHOTS

A Digital Chapbook Series

Nocturne Trio by Metta Sáma

[ART BY MIHRET DAWIT]

Toward What Is Awful by Dana Guthrie Martin

[ART BY GHANGBIN KIM]

How to Survive a Hotel Fire by Angela Veronica Wong

[ART BY MEGAN LAUREL]

The Blue Teratorn by Dorothea Lasky

[ART BY KAORI MITSUSHIMA]

My Hologram Chamber Is Surrounded by Miles of Snow by Ben Mirov

[IMAGES BY ERIC AMLING]